SAY/MIRROR

THE OPERATING SYSTEM PRINT//DOCUMENT

SAY/MIRROR

ISBN 978-0-9860505-2-7
copyright © 2015 by Juliet P. Howard; 2nd edition © 2016; this / third edition © 2020
interview and backmatter, design and editing © 2013-2020 by Elæ [Lynne DeSilva-Johnson]

is released under a Creative Commons CC-BY-NC-ND (Attribution, Non Commercial, No Derivatives) License: its reproduction is encouraged for academic, personal, and other creative usage from which no profit will accrue.

Complete rules and restrictions are available at:
http://creativecommons.org/licenses/by-nc-nd/3.0/

As of 2020 all of our titles are available for donation-only download via our Open Access Library:http://www.theoperatingsystem.org/os-open-access-community-publications-library/

For additional questions regarding reproduction, quotation, or with other requests contact **operator@theoperatingsystem.org**

Cover photo: Ruth King, courtesy of the author

This text was set in Minion Pro, Franchise, 1942 Report and OCR A Standard.
Operating System books in limited edition and small run are printed and bound by Spencer Printing, in Honesdale, PA, in the USA, with distribution to the trade and POD via Ingram.

THE OPERATING SYSTEM//PRESS
141 Spencer Street #203
Brooklyn, NY 11205
www.theoperatingsystem.org

say/mirror
POEMS AND HISTORIES

JP Howard

Winner of the 2016 Lambda Literary Judith A. Markowitz Emerging Writer Award
Finalist for the 2016 Lambda Literary Award for Outstanding Lesbian Poetry

In loving memory of Ruth King 7.31.23 – 12.1.15

Dear Mama,

it has been two months since you left the physical world. i miss every damn thing about you Mama. you are physically gone, but your Diva spirit lives on. Mama, this book is legacy and i'm so glad you lived to see your gorgeous photo on the cover. at 92, I will always treasure your reaction when you first held a copy of say/mirror; how you smiled and said "Damn, I look good!" Mama, this book is Diva love. is complicated like you were. is love and joy and tears and pain. Mama thank you for always loving me, even through your sadness and then again, through your joy. thank you for showing me that it's ok to be a Mama and a Diva simultaneously. thank you for being my praise poem. and for those vintage modeling pictures of you strutting across runways. you will forever be my Diva. thank you for loving boldly. for speaking up and speaking out. for teaching me the power of my voice. every time i speak out against injustice, i hear your big Mama voice pushing me forward. thank you for that big, bold Leo personality. it saved us both, when i was growing up. thank you for being my first and fiercest advocate. you believed in me and now i believe in me. thank you for teaching me to take risks, by your own actions. thank you for all that gorgeous Mama love. i carry it deep, deep in my heart Mama.

Love,

Your baby girl,
Juliet

February 2016

Ruth King winning a costume prize at the Urban League Ball at the Savoy Ballroom in Harlem. New York, February 1949. Photographer: Yale Joel

Recognition/Acknowledgements:

I have so much gratitude for my mother, Ruth King, who really is the inspiration for SAY/MIRROR. My perspective is unique, as I grew up in Sugar Hill, Harlem with a mother who was well known for being a model, long before she became a mother. It took some time for her to transition from being a Diva into being a Mom, but ultimately it was a role she lovingly grew into. My Mom has always been my earliest and biggest advocate, a true Leo lioness who always had my back. I am so grateful for my sweet family who continues to support and inspire me on a daily basis, especially my life partner, Norma Jean Jennings. Our two sons, Jordan and Nicholas Howard-Jennings, have made being a Mom probably the best job in the world.

Special thanks to Pam Laskin, my good friend, who believed in this manuscript from the very first time she read it and worked hard to help me find a home for SAY/MIRROR. Huge thanks to Lynne DeSilva-Johnson, who has been the best editor/publisher/everywoman anyone could ever ask for. Thank you for helping make my vision become a reality!

Finally, there are too many names to list here, but so much of my life is about collaboration and community who lift me up. I am especially grateful to my Women Writers in Bloom Poetry Salon (WWBPS) community who inspire me every month, as well as to the beautiful poets who continue to write and exchange poetry with me on an ongoing basis these last few years, the ability to exchange poetry weekly and get feedback is invaluable.

-Juliet P. Howard

VERSIONS OF THESE POEMS HAVE
PREVIOUSLY APPEARED IN THE FOLLOWING:

what mama served up, MiPOesias iPad Companion Nov. 2012

Family Secret, Cave Canem Anthology XII, 2012 Willow Books
[an Imprint of Aquarius Press]

Praise Poem for the Journey, The Mom Egg, 2013 Vol.11
Mother Tongue

Ghazal for Her Voice, Adrienne A Poetry Journal of Queer Women,
Sibling Rivalry Press, Issue 01, January 2014

Diva Doll, Nepantla: A Journal Dedicated to Queer Poets of Color,
September 2014

Praise Poem for our Mamas, The Americas Poetry Festival of New York
2014: Multilingual Anthology, Artepoética Press Inc.

Ghazal: What Love Takes, Muzzle Magazine (online) and Muzzle
Magazine's Best of the First Year Print Issue (2011)

*When your Mama is a Leo Diva; Ghazal for your eyes only;
love note to a poem; For the Poet, Pat Parker, on saving lives; and
Dear Moon;* in the chaplet "bury your love poems here"
(Belladonna* Collaborative, 2015)

REMEMBERING: A PREFACE — 11
PRAISE POEM FOR TODAY — 19
WHEN YOUR MAMA IS A LEO DIVA — 21
ARCHAEOLOGY — 22
GHAZAL: WHAT LOVE TAKES — 23
DRESS UP — 24
ATLANTIC CITY — 25
DIVA DOLL — 27
GOOD HAIR (FOR MAYA) — 30
SLANTED PRAISE POEM for BABYGIRL — 31
FAMILY SECRET — 32
ON FALLING IN LOVE WITH WORDS — 33
LITTLE GIRL VOICE — 34
PRAISE POEM FOR THE JOURNEY — 35
SECRETS: AFTER AN ETHEREE — 36
I AM GOOD AT SECRETS — 37
WHAT MAMA SERVED UP — 38
SAY/MIRROR — 40
BY THE BAY — 41
GHAZAL FOR HER VOICE — 42
BLUE — 43
PRAISE POEM FOR OUR MAMAS — 44
NINETY — 46
SUBTEXTS: A ZUIHITSU — 47
ON BECOMING WHOLE : AFTER AUDRE LORDE — 49
FOR THE POET, PAT PARKER, ON SAVING LIVES — 50
GHAZAL FOR YOUR EYES ONLY — 51
DEAR MOON, — 52
LOVE NOTE TO A POEM — 53
WHAT TO SAY TO A FRIEND WHO WANTS TO GIVE UP — 54
NOTES AND COMMENTARY — 55

Ruth King (3rd from right) with Cab Calloway, Sugar Ray Robinson and others. Date and photographer unknown.

Remembering: A Preface

Growing up in Sugar Hill, Harlem on 149th Street right off of Convent Avenue was like having my very own history book as my backyard. I don't think there was ever a time when my Mama wasn't telling me/teaching me about the Harlem Renaissance and all the great folks that had contributed so much culture to our beloved neighborhood before I was even born. And then there was Mama the Diva, the one and only Ruth King. There were always pictures of my Mama in our cramped apartment. There were hundreds of pictures of Mama, who had been a well known runway model in Harlem, before she had me.

The pictures were from the 1940's and 1950's and they were glamorous. I realized at a very young age there was never a camera that didn't love Mama and Mama never met a camera she didn't love. Some of my poems explore my own love/hate relationship with the camera and Mama.

Mama spoke honestly about what it meant for her to be a model in Harlem and often talked about how she had "broken the barrier." She explained that she was one of the first brown skinned models who did not have straight or white folks hair and who gained notoriety as an African American model. I learned that before she came along most Black models were very light skinned, some almost to the point that they could pass as white women and most of them had long straight hair. She explained to me that this was the beauty ideal that was strutting on runways, so when she came along with her tantalizing brown skin, her Black folks hair, that was not straight and did not hang down her back, there was agitation in the modeling community. What was clear to me was that Mama was a trailblazer who did not step off the runway because she did not look like the African American models that had long dominated the runways before her arrival. She was gorgeous, other folks knew she was stunning and her Leo ego was strong enough to sustain herself and ignore folks who didn't appreciate all her fabulousness. There were pictures of her on magazine covers that showed she was Harlem's most eligible bachelorette and that she traveled in circles with famous Black politicians and other celebrities, so it was clear she had successfully "broken the barrier" and was paving the way for African American models of all gorgeous shades to also strut their stuff on the runway. Years later when she was interviewed for the coffee table book *Skin Deep: Inside the World of Black Fashion Models* by Barbara Summers (Harpers Collins, 1998) this was confirmation that she had indeed broken the barrier and was recognized as a Black fashion model by a larger audience. Here is a link to the picture included in the book, now on vintage black glamour: *http://vintageblackglamour.tumblr.com/post/11403462429ruth-king-a-popular-1950s-model-on-the-runway*

This book is really an extension of me, as daughter, as mother, as woman finding her voice. *SAY/MIRROR* – the title reflects a dual reality, one is the narrator looking in the Mirror

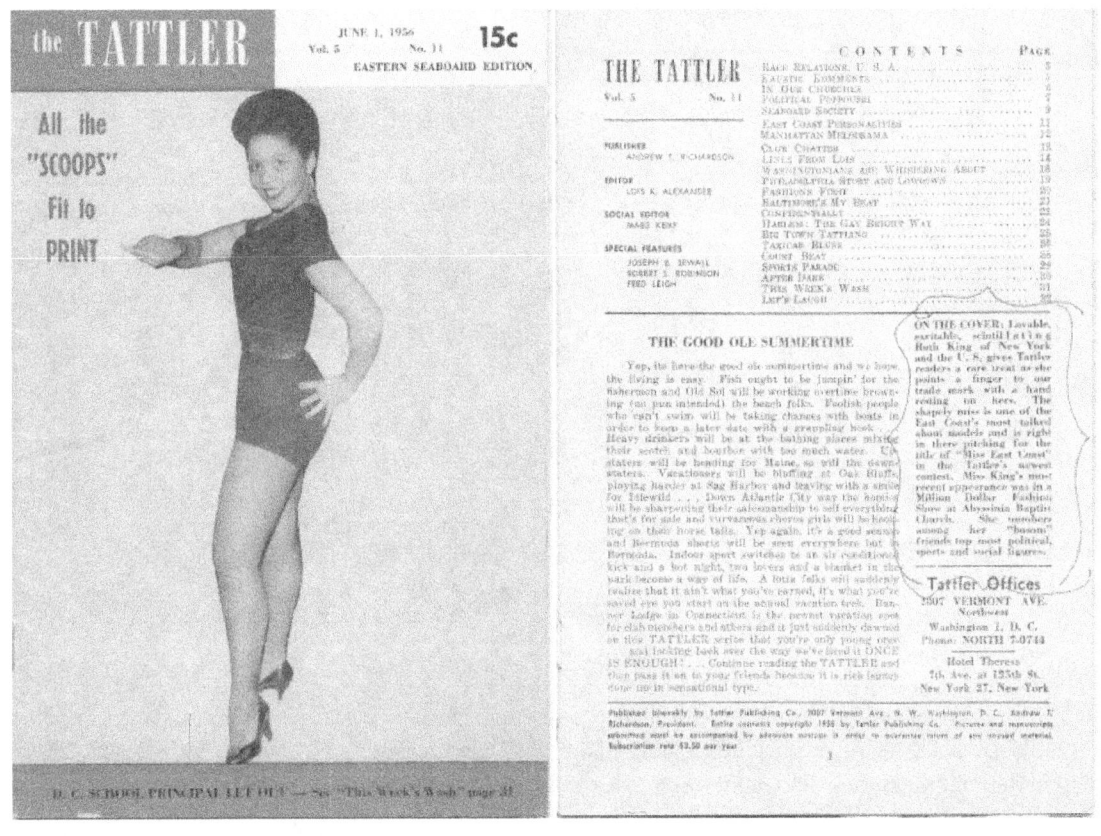

Both pages, L-R, all Ruth King: SEPIA RECORD Cover, date unknown; Calendar Girl, 1948; The TATTLER Cover 1956

and using her voice to explore both history and present day, often through the lens of the mother/daughter relationship. There is also the Mirror as symbolic, since my mother was a Model there were always Mirror(s) which filled our home and the title plays with the idea of self as mirror/as reflection as well as Mama who sometimes saw her child as object/as doll/as her own mirror/something/someone she had created and could show and tell. There is also my mother who by breaking the "color" barrier, had something to say to the Mirror. While my mother was darker complexioned than Black models before her and her presence on the runways was ground breaking because of that, there was a flip side that played into our relationship. Ironically, as her daughter, I had features that one would associate with the light skinned models who were given preference during that era; those fair skinned Black women with what society called "good hair" and who Black folks described as "high yellow."

My mother and many of her friends would often praise me because of my lighter skin and "good hair." My mother greatly valued how I was perceived by society, especially within our Harlem neighborhood, where neighbors were quick to touch my hair, complement me on my light skin and constantly reinforce these ridiculous, deep-seated ideas of beauty. My mother made sure I did child modeling and often treated me as her "doll", always dressing me up with frills, bows, taffeta, lots of pink and girly outfits as a sort of "show and tell." She always wanted my hair long and flowing and when I finally cut it short as a teenager, she was devastated.

It was clear she had put many of society's ideas of beauty onto me. While she encouraged and consistently supported my academics, she also put great emphasis on the physical nature of my appearance, so much so that I sometimes felt objectified. While my mother eventually grew into her role as mother, there were times when I was younger that she put great value on how I looked, perhaps because she was a model and was constantly bombarded with images of beauty. I've never really discussed this aspect of our relationship with my mother; yet this was an issue that was very real for me growing up in Harlem.

Poetry has been played a pivotal role in my life since childhood. I recall being around the same

This page: 9 yo IP Howard poses in Harlem studio, photographer Austin Hansen. . Right: : Howard, 7 y.o. on the runway.

age as my ten year old son is now, and my mother having me recite to the church ladies after church each Sunday, Margaret Walker's poem "For My People." I absolutely loved that poem and the reaction my mother and the ladies would have which was always positive and encouraging. I was painfully shy in my everyday life, but when I recited poetry, it helped to build up my self confidence. It allowed me to become comfortable with my voice.

Over the years, poetry has become an integral part of most aspects of my life. I curate and nurture Women Writers in Bloom Poetry Salon (WWBPS), a monthly Literary Salon Series based in New York. We will celebrate our fourth year in 2015. The goal of the Salon was to create a safe and supportive space to nurture women writers and to come together monthly in the intimacy of folks homes to write, fellowship, discover new poets and their work. The Salon has grown tremendously since it was founded in 2011 and in the process, I have learned so much about myself as a community organizer. Poetry is like air for poets, we need it to breathe, to express our views, frustrations, to praise folks and as a way to protest and to love. I think there has been such amazing community interest and participation in the Salon because I have, through the participation of community, created a sacred space each time we come together to write and share new words. It is transformative, even when we are writing about the most difficult and painful and timely topics, because of the safe community where our words are exchanged. I am surrounded by poets, not just in my Salon, but in my family and amongst my close friends. Both my sons are talented poets. Nicholas, my 10 year old, often collaborates with me and is an integral part of my monthly Salon series. I have always seen poetry as political, from when I first discovered poetry back in elementary school, it was clear to me that poets used words to express their frustrations with the state of the world.

Later on, I discovered the poetry of Black lesbian-identified poets such as Pat Parker, Audre Lorde and Cheryl Clarke when I was 18. As a young Black lesbian just beginning to come out to my own family, these lesbian-identified Black poets were unabashed in their love for women and often wrote political poetry on issues of race, gender and sexual orientation. Discovering their work at that point in my life was seminal. I realized that I too could write about whatever topic I wanted without fear or shame. My recent participation in the *#BlackPoetsSpeakOut* Movement, puts me in the long line of literary tradition of Black poets, Queer and otherwise, who have used poetry to participate in justice movements.

JP Howard and her family

SAY/MIRROR

PRAISE POEM FOR TODAY

Praise the first poet you ever read.
Praise Mama who asked you to recite her favorite Margaret Walker poem,
to church ladies at Abyssinian every Sunday,
when you were in elementary school.
Praise sound of your voice then and now.
Praise your inner child and her will to live.
Praise Mama's cycle of sadness.
Praise all those tears you shed.
Praise that couple who cried when they heard your Trayvon poems.
Praise black boys you wrap in stanzas.
Praise sons who live on through candlelight vigils.
Praise your shattered past and your unknown future.
Praise sweet sound of words on your tongue before they stain the sheet.
Praise poets who split themselves open to save lives.
Praise all the poems you don't want to write, but will, to save your own life.
Praise secrets that burn the page.
Praise ex-lovers who will never die as long as you write.
Praise beauty of a new poem pushing her way to surface.
Praise her shape on the page as she unfolds.

WHEN YOUR MAMA IS A LEO DIVA

1. You can't help but be a Diva yourself.
2. Sometimes she forget she a Mama; she never forget she a Diva.
3. She will tell you you're the most beautiful person in the room; you will believe her.
4. At 90 she still fine and wears ruby red lipstick when she enters a room.
5. She will never forgive you for cutting your long hair nearly 25 years ago.
6. She will tell you how gorgeous every new haircut looks on you, followed by
"despite the fact that you cut your beautiful, long hair off decades ago."
7. She will teach you the art of self-love and self-care, before you go to middle school.
8. She will not learn how to cook until you leave for college
and have no regrets about serving you shake and bake all those years.
9. She will be your biggest advocate and sometimes your greatest obstacle.
10. She will love you, even you when you have stopped loving yourself.

ARCHAEOLOGY

when I say poem,
I mean forgiving mama
soundless nights
passed out on bed.

when I say forgiving mama,
I mean tucking her in between
stanzas until we both find sleep.

when I say sleep,
I mean unearthing
childhood skeletons.

when I say skeletons,
I mean body craving
touch of skin before bone.

when I say craving,
I mean lover loss
memory filling space.

when I say lover,
I mean touch find
work my way
into the poem.

GHAZAL: WHAT LOVE TAKES

I'm sleeping as I write this; you're standing over me crying
while Ella belts out: *No, no they can't take that away from me*

if this is all I can get, your hand on my shoulder in the dream,
lips warm against my neck, *I'll take that*

the alarm clock becomes enemy; I press snooze every few minutes,
search for you and finally press stop when I can't take it any more

please don't mistake this for a love poem – I stopped writing those
damn things once you left; anyhow, that last poem I wrote: you wouldn't take it

I call my mama and ask her how she lived all those decades
knowing her lover would never fully be hers and she said: *chile, you just take it*

wake up! rewind routine daily, tuck kids in, cook dinner work round the clock,
leave patience on the dining room table while making breakfast, and the kids take it

as I wake from the dream, your tears fall from my eyes and I ask myself:
J why do you complicate love? why can't you just take it?

DRESS UP

if I could hold memory this would be the snapshot: babygirl, happy with yourself, a splash of pastels: powder blue, pale pink, Mama's lemon striped dress falling off your shoulders. Isn't that her sunday best wig, under that big church hat? tilted, tipped, tickling, you all giggles going on an adventure through your Sugar Hill apartment all those oversized Mama bags packed for the trip those French doors leading to a land faraway

ATLANTIC CITY

before there were casinos lining the boardwalk,
this was our space:
each summer's rented
pale pink bedroom, round carnation bed
and oval windows, circling around.
just a jitney ride from the boardwalk.

this was our ritual:
one week to be just two.

you stayed out your cups that week,
drank coffee with lots of cream, and
even let me try it:
cream and sugar with a hint
of coffee.

I still like it light and sweet.

you tried your best at breakfast,
slimy scrambled eggs that slid off the plate;

I held my breath, gulped that coffee flavored cream
with each bite.

on bikes on the boardwalk each day
how funny you looked, all
high-heeled mules
rhinestone sunglasses
and dangling gold hoop earrings,
that rattled the whole ride from Atlantic City to Ventnor.

stuffed on frozen custard and Fralinger's salt water taffy
every day the man in the Mr. Peanut suit standing in front of the Planters' store
waved at us, but never said a word.
you let me win the arcade games, mama, taught me
how to angle my arm to get the
highest skee-ball score
and after, in the cabana on the beach,
the smell of salt water lulled us to sleep.

DIVA DOLL

Mama was a Diva.
Mama's baby was a living doll.
Baby doll.
Barbie doll.
Mama collected dolls.
Pale pink porcelain dolls.
Mama dressed her dolls.
Mama dressed her baby girl
like her dolls.
Powder puff pink
Show and Tell baby doll.
Show and Tell, Baby Girl.
Mama's baby girl.
Mama's baby doll.
Painted porcelain face dolls.
Puckered ruby lips dolls.
Ebony eyeliner etched around hollow eyes dolls.
Cinnamon blush circling cheekbones dolls.
Glossy. Glossy. Flash. Flash. Flash.
Cameras loved Mama

almost as much as
Mama loved cameras.
Smile real pretty for the camera baby.
Walk down the runway baby girl.
Strut your stuff like Mama.
Follow Mama. Follow Mama.
Follow Diva.
Mama planted cherry blossom pink barrettes seeds in baby girl's ponytails.
Dressed baby girl up pretty like her dolls.
Candy coated, sealed in a rainbow of pink.
Mama wrapped her baby girl in slivers of coral, cerise, magenta,
fragments of a pale pink
Tree Swallow's eggshell.
Mama loved shiny.
Shiny objects. Shiny surfaces.
Shiny dolls.
Dolls wrapped in plastic boxes.
Mama's trophies.
Mama's Show and Tell.
Show and Tell, Mama.
Mama posed for pictures.

Mama loved studio shots.
Smile real pretty baby.
Smile big like Mama.
You look like a living doll.
Pictures don't lie.
Hollow eyes peering from behind porcelain silhouettes.
Eyes don't lie.
Mama hung pictures of baby girl
all around the house.
Mama hung pictures of herself
all around the house.
Baby doll.
Mama doll.
Living dolls.
Pictures filled shelves, walls, framed empty spaces.
Mama's mirror.
Mama buried her baby girl in pale pink lace.
Mama didn't touch.
Mama just carved her baby girl a rose plum clay platform.
Left her there for all to see.

GOOD HAIR (For Maya)

When I was little I wanted to be just like Mama. Oh how I loved her Afro Puffs, so soft and full, how they framed her face just so. I loved her dashikis, in every color imaginable, always fitted at the waist to show her hips. I wanted to look in my mirror and see Mama instead of me.

But Mama saw pretty in my mirror, pink and lavender bows tied lovingly, at the tip of my two stringy braids, the ones that fell all the way down my back.

Mama's friends all told her they liked my good hair, but Mama knew it was her hair I loved the most. Mine was flat and stringy against my head, like the white girls that Grandma cooked and cleaned for all week long.

I couldn't stand those girls. How they took Grandma away from us each week with their straight stringy hair.

Once Mama started braiding my hair like my cousins, I finally started to see pretty in my mirror.

I loved how she sat me between her legs, rubbed my scalp with hair grease, weaved those three tight plaits, two on top of my head and one big one at the base, each with matching barrettes the color of the rainbow. I loved those plaits, even if they did fall flat against my head, not poking high towards the sky like my cousins.

SLANTED PRAISE POEM FOR BABY GIRL

shine on Sunday Buster Brown black patent
distracted from that saccharine dagger smile;
stick thin bony knock kneed spitfire
holding us together

pale bows hugged perfect plaits
near wide open ears
holding words in, folded under skin
letting their edges crawl into crevices

pretty, pink and ruffled
they thought I was too shy --
but that turquoise daisy dotted floral dress
held secrets so big and wide,
all I could do to keep afloat
was carve them under my tongue

FAMILY SECRET

Once
when I was five,
mama almost died.
No, that's not quite right.
Once when I was five, mama
wanted to die. No, that's still not right.
Once when I was five, mama tried to die.
I sat in the corner of her bedroom and searched
in silence for signs of life. The rise and fall of her chest.
The warm breath against my cheek. I'd hoped for the familiar.
But it was all, all foreign. Strange sitting in a familiar place surrounded
by strangers in blue uniforms. Words floating around the room. Pulse.
What a pity. Cute kid. I was there and not there. A part of me left that day.
Once, when I was five, my mama tried to die. Silently, she tried to slip away.
But those strangers, those strange men in blue uniforms found the pulse.
I sat quietly watching the scene. I was in it but not of it. I took it all in.
Inhaled it all. Felt the release in the room once they found the pulse.
That fine line between life and death. The unnamable emotion.
Somewhere between grief and joy. When I was five, my mama
wanted to die but didn't. I found her. I lost her. No, that's not
quite right. I found her. I lost that part of me that was
innocent. I'd lost the mama I'd wanted. When I was five
my mama almost died. When I was five my mama
wanted to die. When I was five my mama tried
to die. When I was five, I was a child.
Once.

ON FALLING IN LOVE WITH WORDS (MY FIRST TIME)

It was hot outside and the sweat tickled my neck as I walked into Hamilton Grange Library
at the tip of 145th and Amsterdam only steps from PS 186 and four blocks from my apartment

pushing hard on the big black doors I was scared of the cool silence that welcomed me once they
opened and I thought about running back into the hot sun but I didn't want to go back home to mama
not yet

walking down the rows the quiet excited me

I stopped at the section titled: BLACK POETS pulled down some books from their shelves and picked a
corner table and Amiri Nikki June Langston Ntozake and Lucille
welcomed me into their world
they used curse words I wasn't allowed to use, but I understood each one and liked how it felt
when I whispered them under my breath just loud enough for only me to hear

they wrote about secrets gave names to their fears
allowed silence to speak her voice
and made me feel alive.

I still don't know how many hours I stayed there
but the sun had set by the time I left

caught up in words placed on a page
which tickled my tongue
made me cry
and gave me strength
to go home again and again
to mama and her sorrow.

LITTLE GIRL VOICE

this poem so quiet,
she sound like my ten-year old self,
tip-toeing around her own thoughts

when no one is listening,
she reads other peoples poems.
like the ones she found at the library

she whispers curse words under breath,
so soft even Mama can't hear

so soft even Mama can't hear
her words. her words so soft they disappear.
she swallow them whole

Child eat those words,
let them fill your belly.

PRAISE POEM FOR THE JOURNEY

Praise the therapist who told me twenty years ago:
You are not your mother, you do not have to be your mother.
Praise the years I spent wanting children,
yet afraid to repeat her mistakes.
Praise my child-self who took care of mama every time she passed out.
Praise my adult-self who feared the burden of "caretaker" yet again.
Praise my intellect for recognizing my fears and facing them head on.
Praise my therapist who let me talk out my fears all those years,
long before I wrapped myself in this mama cloak that fits so well.
Praise my mama who did the best with the skills she had.
Praise the Divas who are sometimes forced to be mamas
and the mamas who give birth to Divas.
Praise them all. Shower them with love and affection.
Praise my sons. Praise the first male children born
after three successive generations of women.
Praise their lean bodies growing up, up each day towards manhood.
Praise the spark in their eyes. Praise their keen intellect and
their giggles that fill my heart. Praise this calm my child-self never knew.
Praise the mothers who love from up close and from afar.
Praise our children who we tuck in each night and
those whose names we wrap in prayer,
no matter where they lay their heads down to sleep.

SECRETS: AFTER AN ETHEREE

> End
> is where
> I began.
> If mama had
> popped more pills that night,
> sometimes I wonder where
> I would have landed, feet first
> or face down on the ground?

I AM GOOD AT SECRETS

I keep secrets.
I collect scraps of whispers and
sew seams around jagged hearts;
anything to bind fragments together.
I carry years of Hush chile and Shhh, keep your bizniz to
yourself.
Some years I embellish my past and others, reduce it to flash-
back.
Today I sit stone still,
hands buried in my backyard,
bits of tongue glistening on freezer floor,
while my body waits to be born.
I am a grown woman,
my body a ball of hide and seek.
I bury myself in air vents.
If you quiet, you will hear crackle of my lungs and
silt of my childhood coursing through veins.
I would smile, but my lips are wired shut.
I am good at secrets.

WHAT MAMA SERVED UP

mama never cooked
just thawed out/ordered in
served up alla her frustrations

lukewarm swanson's salisbury steak
with potato puff
green beans and chocobrownies

I can't stop
cooking the childhood I never had
collardgreensblack-eyedpeassmokedturkey
fried chicken and cakes baked from scratch

but on too tired days I order
my childhood favorite:
shrimp with lobster sauce
from the chinese bodega

mama's passed out
half on the floor
half on the bed

beer cans

half-empty liquor bottles/
that leftover smoke smell
        hovering

me
eating the jumbo shrimp

somedays my craving for chocolate is cheap:
I buy ring dings or big wheels
chocolate with something fake and fluffy inside
to make me forget

mama slept through a whole day of drunk
before she came back

sweets still calm
on crazy days
cheap chocolates remember
mama in her bedroom
snoring loud and hard,

me waiting for the calm
nibbling m&m's   to forget

SAY/MIRROR

dressed in her Sunday best:
baby girl cries in the black and white studio shot,
tears running down her pretty little face:
frilly lace, patent leather and puffy eyes.

Mama on the other side.
Mama out the frame.
Somebody take Mama out the damn frame.
We're at the photographer's studio again.

Look away little girl.
Look away from Mama, child.

See the sad skinny light-skinned girl with good hair.
Pretty bows wrapped around those straight stringy braids.
Somebody's doll baby about to break.

C'mon baby smile for Mama.
You such a pretty little thing.
A thing. In a frame.
Sitting pretty with your little tears.

BY THE BAY

where does mama's mind go when she lets go
babies baptized in the bay or the river
screaming No Mama No please please mama don't let us go

Hush little babies
Don't you cry
Mama gonna sing you a lullaby

mama gone push the pedal real hard, car gonna go real fast
water gonna swallow up; all be gone in the blink of an eye

where does baby go when mama's mind breaks
who puts the puzzle back together
while they lie at the bottom of lakes

Rock-a-Bye Babies
by the bay,
mama gone drop you one by one

you were her sunshine, her only sunshine
you'll never know baby
what made mama come undone

GHAZAL FOR HER VOICE

Life is a circle, woven
around fragments of her voice.

I enter an empty room;
drawn to memory of her voice.

Where would she be today, had I
not cut the cord to my voice?

Tomorrow when she wakes,
I wonder *to whose voice*?

One day I will break this cycle
and silence this shattered voice.

Tonight someone whispered, *Juliet*,
wrapped in echoes of her voice.

BLUE

I am blue,
deep-sea aqua veins
scorching through body.
I am pale crested powder blue jay.
I am Bessie blues
bleeding through walls
during blue-black of night.
I am bruised rainbow,
deep purple hue blue.
I am midnight blue
aglow at night.
In the morning, I am sky-blue
shining your window.
I am blue, black and blue,
bitter blue, cotton candy blue
on your tongue, blue note and gin
all night long, cornflower blue
scribbled on your page.
I am forget-me-not petals,
faded hydrangeas,
stalk of an iris,
still as steel,
true.

PRAISE POEM FOR OUR MAMAS

Praise our Mamas
Praise the ones who loved us fiercely
Praise the ones who left us behind
Praise their bosoms
Praise tears we shed all those years
Praise softness of skin against skin
Praise those who listened again and again
Praise poems we birthed
Praise our ability to forgive
Praise the poet's tears
Praise that sweet child that remains
Praise her soft voice
Praise Mama humming your favorite lullaby
Praise Mamas who shut the door
Praise Mamas whose doors were wide open

Praise "Come here sit on Mama lap baby" Mamas
Praise Mamas who never learned to look beyond their reflection
Praise Mama's reflection
Praise Mama in your mirror
Praise your reflection in your mirror
Praise love's complicated contours
Praise her edges, sharp then soft
Praise Mamas who bend and open to hugs
Praise Mamas who never learned to hug
Praise a laying on of hands, soft like Mama's
Praise your best friend, who nurtures like a Mama
Praise the memory of Mama
Praise that soft spot in your heart
Call her Mama.

NINETY

as complicated as she is beautiful
silver ponytail slicked back
lips still full
on good days Mama is scarlet red pout.

she feels prettiest with dangling hoop earrings:
the bigger the bauble the better.
each visit I ask, what color nail polish Mama?
this week aqua blue is her favorite.

there are no roadmaps for aging Divas
just self-portraits lining walls
costume jewelry overflowing and
full-length minks, frayed now.
it is easier to live in the past
than in an aging body

we talk about
her ex-lover.
what did this man do to hold
that twinkle in her eyes?
forty years after he dies,
she savors his name,
lets it linger on her tongue
those full lips a delicious smile.

SUBTEXTS : A ZUIHITSU

August is the hottest month.

Grandma dropped a little tidbit at dinner, as if to say:
Pass the salt baby.
You know nobody knew your mama was even carrying you;
she wore that big grey wool coat all summer long.

Mama tells stories over and over.
Her favorite, how we met a day late.

August 9th is when her story begins.
She laughs out loud every time she repeats our story.
She repeats our story. Over and over.
Some people's funny is a slit to the throat.

This morning after her c-section
a nurse asked Mama how we both managed last night.

Some secrets should stay buried.
Skip generations.

Error. Typo. Revisionist history.
August 8th is when our story begins.

Oh I haven't seen the little thing yet, Mama said, *I slept straight through the night. Slept like a baby. Hope my baby girl did too. Sure, go get her, bring her in the room.*

"We love because it's the only true adventure." Nikki Giovanni

One man's trash is another man's treasure.

Over forty years later, I pack up our little Sugar Hill apartment.
It is smaller than I remembered.
Our walls are not grey tinted green anymore.
We are always saying goodbye.

I find Mama's little diary calendar in her old oversized gold lamé pocketbook. A little piece of history worn from decades. I recognize Mama's script, loops spectacular and glamorous. Entries etched in pencil. Snippets of days. Tiny brush strokes.

>   *1971 April 6: Juliet didn't eat much. Still has fever. Kept her home.*
>   *1971 April 7: Juliet ate soup with crackers. I think her fever is breaking.*
>   *1971 April 8: Juliet on the mend. Have to go shopping for dinner for the two of us.*

The two of us. Two of us. Mama and me. Me and Mama. Just us.

ON BECOMING WHOLE (FOR A SON) - AFTER AUDRE LORDE

How I felt your presence
each day I blossomed
my body perfect for the first time
round where I had been flat
wide where I had been narrow.
I thought I would burst with your fullness.

How the weeks turned into months.
Each year the promise of summer
reminds me of your arrival in the world.
The air heavy with the scent of the city,
me heavy with the weight of you.
I remember resting often.
Arms legs stretching pushing
those purposeful elbows and knees
prodding, reminding me
daily of a world inside my belly.
Then the waters burst.
I pushed my heart to the surface
on a rain-soaked July morning
and the world was yours.

Today complete
I cannot imagine
this space without you.
You, unfolding
into Yourself.

FOR THE POET, PAT PARKER
ON SAVING LIVES

For the poet, Pat Parker, on saving lives

Some poets make magic.
They write real shyt,
save li(f)e of a teen
who buries herself under covers.

Their poems sp(l)it in your mouth.
If you ain't careful,
they will tongue kiss you
while you sleep.

GHAZAL FOR YOUR EYES ONLY

I will pretend you were dream,
you will walk through me, eyes closed.

Swing me dizzy in wide circles,
then fall onto me, giddy, your eyes closed.

When you blink, ten years will pass,
in the end remember me, my eyes closed.

Sometimes a voice splits us.
You can see her silhouette with your eyes closed.

Mama had a secret lover for three decades,
she buried him in vodka with eyes closed.

Do you remember our first kiss?
How you whispered Jules, both our eyes closed.

DEAR MOON,

You are exquisite.
Some nights you are a perfect sphere,
a magic hand out my window.
On others you are sliver of light,
stunning against blue-black of night.

Sometimes you are brilliant, a ball of sparkle,
in reach of my grasp.
You follow me through years,
hold secrets deep in crevices.
Do you remember that first night I kissed her?

You, a perfect half-circle,
her face aglow in your shadow.
Sweet Moon, sometimes you are cruel with your games.
You were full, almost bursting, that night of our last kiss.
Still, you are divine, during dead silence of night.

When I am lonely, I curl myself up,
my body aglow against your crescent.
Your shadow a soft trigger,
a scorching kiss, a goodbye,
a burst of night.

LOVE NOTE TO A POEM

dear poem,

thank you for finding me.
i was getting tired of all those secrets, now you let them fly off the page.
they beautiful when they transform and flutter.
poem, sometimes you sound like my 6th grade teacher, mr. jamison,
right after i told him my secret, that papa had died the night before,
that mama drank her smirnoff and was too drunk to know any better,
so she sent me to school anyhow.
poem, sometimes you sound like him, your voice deep yet soft,
whispering, you so strong baby girl, you stronger than even you know.
poem sometimes you a wreath of sunflowers.

love,
me

WHAT TO SAY TO A FRIEND WHO WANTS TO GIVE UP

Say I love you, even when you can't love yourself.
Say please, please not today,
Say too much life unlived.
Say mirror, say beautiful,
Say this arm, take this arm,
Say grab, say hold, say let tears fall,
Say tears heal, Say forgive your mama,
Say she did the best she could.
Say tomorrow, say sleep,
Say split second, split the seconds,
Say let the seconds turn into days,
Say today, Say tomorrow, Say sun.
Say warm, Say skin,
Say warm skin, say sunlight,
Say new day, Say breath,
Say inhale, Say exhale.
Say not today baby girl,
Say so much life to live,
Say love, Say I love you.
Say hold on, hold on to love.

notes and commentary

clockwise from top left:
Ruth King with Eartha Kitt,
Ruth King with Richard Nixon,
JP Howard in her childhood home

POET JP HOWARD
and EDITOR
LYNNE DESILVA-JOHNSON
IN CONVERSATION

Who are you?
I am a mom, a lover, a poet, a curator and nurturer of all things poetry.

Why are you a poet?
I am a poet because poetry helps me stay connected to the world and express myself.
It's the lens through which I view the world.

When did you decide you were a poet?
I was in elementary school definitely. Maybe 8 or 9 years old.

What's a "poet"?
A poet is someone who has the courage to speak the truth as they see or experience it.

What is the role of the poet today?
The poet has many roles, currently I see the role of the poet as educator,
as political activist, as lover of words and ideas.

What do you see as your cultural and social role?
(in the poetry community and beyond)

My cultural role and social role is as community organizer/curator/nurturer. I think I am a natural leader, perhaps true to my Leo sign. I am most comfortable as collaborator and I work well with others to effectuate change. It's a strength I've become more aware of and truly embraced these past, nearly three years, curating the Salon and working with a larger community.

Why did you decide to create a book from your work?

I've been writing different versions of this book my whole life.

I especially started focusing on this particular version after my mom gave me a ton of her vintage black and white modeling photos from the 1940's and 1950's a few years back and this really 1) mesmerized me, because some of the pictures I hadn't seen previously and they were stunning and 2) I began to think a lot about how beauty and how the lens through which I saw my mom, growing up, in her shadow so to speak, affected me. The poems began to unfold the more I let myself explore that part of myself.

What does this particular collection of poems represent to you
-- as representative of your method/practice:
-- as representative of your history:

The poems are definitely like a lens which allow me to look back on my childhood, but also look forward and see where I was and how both my mom and I have evolved. They are like a kaleidoscope through which fragments of my life are turning, but on the page.

-- as representative of your beliefs:

While some of the poems are a bit dark, sharing "childhood secrets" or events society tells us not to traditionally write about, I am all about being open and I view poetry as cathartic, so in that sense these poems represent my belief that writing brings us towards healing.

How is this collection representative of your mission/intentions/hopes/plans....?

The poems support my vision that poetry can tell complicated stories within a narrow frame. I also have a creative non-fiction/memoir type book that I am working on right now, so SAY/MIRROR is a small, but important way for me to explore my sometimes complicated mother/daughter relationship.

Talk a little bit about method, form, and writing process. How are the poems in this book representative of your practice and/or the history of your practice?

Some of these poems were written when I had fellowships at Cave Canem or Lambda Literary Foundation and a number were written during National Poetry Month poetry exchange groups which I am a part of, which have extended years after NaPoMo ended. I enjoy writing in form, though many of the poems in this collection loosely use form.

How do we see your development as a poet through these poems?

Some first drafts of these poems were written a number of years ago, and many of the final versions have changed with time and editing. I think poems, just like people evolve and mature with time and life experience.

What formal structures or other constrictive processes do you use in the creation of your work?

Diva Doll was initially written in the summer of 2012 in Los Angeles at a Lambda Writers Retreat for Emerging LGBT Voices in a workshop with our fierce facilitator Jewelle Gomez. There have been numerous revisions and edits in the few years since, but the overall pace and intention of the poem has not changed. The prompt for the poem was the picture of a Black Barbie doll, a collectors item, dressed in an original Bob Mackie gown that a friend had given me some years ago. Jewelle had told us before we came to California for the retreat to bring pictures that had some meaning to us and one had to be an object, so that was my object. The prompt to write about that object pushed me to write Diva Doll and also I ended up creating a poetry video collage using that doll and my mom's black and white photos.

The poem Family Secret was one of the most difficult poems I have ever written. I wrote the initial draft during a Cave Canem retreat in 2009. Toi Derricotte suggested a prompt, which was to write about a family secret – preferably about something we had never written about ever before. That night I went back to my room on campus and wrote Family Secret, which was literally a family memory that I had never written about previously. I remember staying up to 3 or 4am in the morning working on that poem in the dorm at the University of Pittsburgh and my two closest Cave Canem friends came out to check on me. I recall literally reading it to them and crying as I read it. I both loved and hated that poem. I had never written about that childhood memory of finding my mother, passed out and the EMT workers trying to revive her. I was really scared to turn it in for my assignment the next morning, but I did.

My friends encouraged me and it was a defining moment for me as a poet. If I could write about that HUGE family secret and still live and not explode, I figured there were other things I could also write about. Dynamic poet and Professor Ed Roberson was my instructor and gave such positive feedback on that poem. He explained it was essentially a litany, because of the repetition and form and also like a dirge, because there was a mourning for the loss of the innocence of the child and he felt it worked really well. Another student ran out of class in tears because that poem had touched something in her. It was both terrifying and cathartic to share that poem and also I experienced a bit of the same feelings when deciding whether to include it in this manuscript.

There is this "taboo" particularly in the Black community, about airing our "dirty laundry" and this poem felt a bit like that. However, the reality is that depression knows no color, race, sexual orientation or age and can affect any and everyone. I'm sure many adults have a childhood memory they may be encouraged to keep hidden, so this poem is for all those people holding in those secrets.

Let's talk a little bit about the role of poetics and creative community in social activism, in particular in what I call "Civil Rights 2.0," what we're going through now as this book nears publication. Can you tell me about your engagement in #blackpoetsspeakout, for instance?

I'd also be curious to hear some thoughts on the challenges we face in speaking and publishing across lines of race, age, privilege, social/cultural background, and sexuality within the creative community vs. the danger of remaining and producing in isolated silos.

The #BlackPoetsSpeakOut movement is a way for me to stay connected to the long line of poets who have been a part of justice movements. It has also been a way for me, as the Mom of two school age Black sons, and one a teenager, to express my rage, my anger, my dismay with the current state of the world, particularly continued examples of racial injustice and police brutality against young African American men and women. Every time a Black youth is killed I find myself first reacting as mother, then as a poet. This poetic movement allows me to continue to use my poetry to mourn, to protest, to wish for peace and to fight for justice.

When I think about the challenges of speaking/publishing/representing all parts of my self, I often think of the words of the late poet, Pat Parker, who said in her book *Movement in Black*:

"If I could take all my parts with me when I go somewhere, and not have to say to one of them, "No, you stay home tonight, you won't be welcome," because I'm going to an all-white party where I can be gay, but not Black. Or I'm going to a Black poetry reading, and half the poets are antihomosexual, or thousands of situations where something of what I am cannot come with me. The day all the different parts of me can come along, we would have what I would call a revolution."

I am always aware of wearing multiple hats, I am Black lesbian, poet, partner, mother, daughter, community organizer and advocate. Like Parker, I strive to bring all parts of myself to the table when I show up; yet I also know that some parts of me are more welcome than others, depending on the forum or audience I am addressing. That being said, my goal is to not let other peoples issues, phobias and/or "isms" keep me from bringing my whole complicated poetic self to the table.

Ruth King at a cricket game, Hamilton, Bermuda, circa 1950's.

photo: Nivea Castro

JP Howard aka Juliet P. Howard

JULIET P HOWARD aka JP HOWARD is a Cave Canem graduate fellow. She is the author of SAY/MIRROR, a debut poetry collection published by The Operating System (2015) and a chaplet "bury your love poems here" (Belladonna Collaborative*, 2015). She curates Women Writers in Bloom Poetry Salon (WWBPS), a forum offering women writers a venue to come together in a positive and supportive space in NY. The Salon celebrates a diverse array of women poets and includes a large LGBTQ POC membership. JP is an alum of the VONA/Voices Writers Workshop, as well as a Lambda Literary Foundation Emerging LGBT Voices Fellow. She was a finalist in The Feminist Wire's 2014 1st Poetry Contest. Her poems have appeared or are forthcoming in The Feminist Wire, pluck! The Journal of Affrilachian Arts & Culture, Poets, Split this Rock, Nepantla: A Journal for Queer Poets of Color, Muzzle Magazine, Adrienne: A Poetry Journal of Queer Women, The Best American Poetry Blog, MiPOesias, The Mom Egg, Talking Writing and Connotation Press, among others. JP holds an MFA in Creative Writing from the City College of New York and a BA from Barnard College.

/////THE OPERATING SYSTEM IS A QUESTION, NOT AN ANSWER.

THIS is not a fixed entity.

The OS is an ongoing experiment in resilient creative practice which necessarily morphs as its conditions and collaborators change. It is not a magazine, a website, or a press, but rather an ongoing dialogue ABOUT the act of publishing on and offline: it is an exercise in the use and design of both of these things and their role in our shifting cultural landscape, explored THROUGH these things.

I see publication as documentation: an act of resistance, an essential community process, and a challenge to the official story / archive, and I founded the OS to exemplify my belief that people everywhere can train themselves to use self or community documentation as the lifeblood of a resilient, independent, successful creative practice.

The name "`THE OPERATING SYSTEM`" is meant to speak to an understanding of the self as a constantly evolving organism, which just like any other system needs to learn to adapt if it is to survive. Just like your computer, you need to be "updating your software" frequently, as your patterns and habits no longer serve you.

Our intentions above all are empowerment and unsilencing, encouraging creators of all ages and colors and genders and backgrounds and disciplines to reclaim the rights to cultural storytelling, and in so doing to the historical record of our times and lives.

Bob Holman once told me I was "scene agnostic" and I took this as the highest compliment: indeed, I seek work and seek to make and promote work that will endure and transcend tastes and trends, making important and asserting value rather than being told was has and has not.

The OS has evolved in quite a short time from an idea to a growing force for change and possibility: in a span of 5 years, from 2013-2017, we will have published more than 40 volumes from a hugely diverse group of contributors, and solicited and curated thousands of pieces online, collaborating with artists, composers, choreographers, scientists, futurists, and so many more. Online, you'll also find partnerships with cultural organizations modelling the value of archival process documentation.

Beginning in 2016, our new series :: "Glossarium: Unsilenced Texts and Modern Translations", will bring on Ariel Resnikoff, Stephen Ross, and Mona Kareem as contributing editors, and have as its first volume a dual language translation of Palestinian poet and artist Ashraf Fayadh's "Instructions Within," translated by Mona Kareem, which will be published later this year, with all proceeds going to support Fayadh's ongoing case and imprisonment in Saudi Arabia.

There is ample room here for you to expand and grow your practice ...and your possibility. Join us.

- *Lynne DeSilva-Johnson, Founder and Managing Editor*

TITLES IN THE PRINT: DOCUMENT COLLECTION

In Corpore Sano : Creative Practice and the Challenged Body [Anthology, 2016]
Lynne DeSilva-Johnson and Jay Besemer, co-editors

Instructions Within [2016] - Ashraf Fayadh
Arabic-English dual language edition; Mona Kareem, translator

Let it Die Hungry [2016] - Caits Meissner

Everything is Necessary [2016] - Keisha-Gaye Anderson

agon [2016] - Judith Goldman

Everybody's Automat [2016] - Mark Gurarie

How to Survive the Coming Collapse of Civilization [2016] - Sparrow

CHAPBOOK SERIES 2016: OF SOUND MIND
*featuring the quilt drawings of Daphne Taylor
Improper Maps - Alex Crowley; While Listening - Alaina Ferris;
Chords - Peter Longofono; Any Seam or Needlework - Stanford Cheung

TEN FOUR - Poems, Translations, Variations [2015]- Jerome Rothenberg, Ariel Resnikoff, Mikhl Likht

MARILYN [2015] - Amanda Ngoho Reavey

CHAPBOOK SERIES 2015: OF SYSTEMS OF
*featuring original cover art by Emma Steinkraus
Cyclorama - Davy Knittle; The Sensitive Boy Slumber Party Manifesto - Joseph Cuillier;
Neptune Court - Anton Yakovlev; Schema - Anurak Saelow

SAY/MIRROR [2015; 2nd edition 2016] - JP HOWARD

Moons Of Jupiter/Tales From The Schminke Tub [plays] - Steve Danziger

CHAPBOOK SERIES 2014: BY HAND
Pull, A Ballad - Maryam Parhizkar; Executive Producer Chris Carter - Peter Milne Grenier;
Spooky Action at a Distance - Gregory Crosby; Can You See that Sound - Jeff Musillo

CHAPBOOK SERIES 2013: WOODBLOCK
*featuring original prints from Kevin William Reed
Strange Coherence - Bill Considine;; The Sword of Things - Tony Hoffman;
Talk About Man Proof - Lancelot Runge / John Kropa;
An Admission as a Warning Against the Value of Our Conclusions -Alexis Quinlan

DOC U MENT
/däkyəmənt/

First meant "instruction" or "evidence," whether written or not.

noun - a piece of written, printed, or electronic matter that provides information or evidence or that serves as an official record
verb - record (something) in written, photographic, or other form
synonyms - paper - deed - record - writing - act - instrument

[Middle English, precept, from Old French, from Latin *documentum*, example, proof, from *docre*, to teach; see *dek-* in Indo-European roots.]

Who is responsible for the manufacture of value?
Based on what supercilious ontology have we landed in a space where we vie against other creative people in vain pursuit of the fleeting credibilities of the scarcity economy, rather than freely collaborating and sharing openly with each other in ecstatic celebration of MAKING?

While we understand and acknowledge the economic pressures and fear-mongering that threatens to dominate and crush the creative impulse, we also believe that now more than ever we have the tools to relinquish agency via cooperative means,
fueled by the fires of the Open Source Movement.

Looking out across the invisible vistas of that rhizomatic parallel country
we can begin to see our community beyond constraints,
in the place where intention meets resilient, proactive, collaborative organization.

Here is a document born of that belief, sown purely of imagination and will.
When we document we assert. We print to make real, to reify our being there.
When we do so with mindful intention to address our process,
to open our work to others, to create beauty in words in space, to respect and acknowledge the strength of the page we now hold physical, a thing in our hand...
we remind ourselves that, like Dorothy: *we had the power all along, my dears.*

THE PRINT! DOCUMENT SERIES
is a project of
the trouble with bartleby

in collaboration with
the operating system

www.ingramcontent.com/pod-product-compliance
Lightning Source LLC
Chambersburg PA
CBHW080520300426
44112CB00018B/2809